The Local Legacy of
Thomas Cook

Derek Seaton

The statue of Thomas Cook outside London Road Railway Station, Leicester

The Local Legacy of
Thomas Cook

Derek Seaton

First published 1996 by D.Seaton
Botcheston, Leics.
© Copyright

British Library Cataloguing in Publication Data. A catalogue record for this book is available from the British Library.

By the same author:

Light amid the Shadows
The History of the Royal Leicestershire, Rutland and Wycliffe Society for the Blind 1858-1993

ISBN 0 9528948 0 7

Front cover:
The portrait of Thomas Cook is reproduced by kind permission of Thomas Cook Travel Archive, 45 Berkeley Street, London W1A 1EB.

Printed in Great Britain by Norwood Press, Anstey, Leics.
Designed by Birdhouse, Leicester.

Foreword

Derek Seaton has immersed himself in the story of the local connections of a man born the only son of a poor villager, who left school at the age of ten to hawk vegetables and plants around his home area for a penny a day, but had the inborn gift which led to world-wide fame, not only for his adventurous exploration and early development of the possibilities of travel, his thought for the poor, the deprived and the alcoholic, but also as a lay preacher with his concern for the well-being of the whole man.

This may not be the first book to tell of Thomas Cook, but in its presentation it must stand alone. "Charms strike the sight, but merit wins the soul" - so wrote Alexander Pope. Derek Seaton has assuredly succeeded in both.

ER Frizelle DSc MCh FRCS
Surgeon emeritus and historiographer
Leicester Royal Infirmary.

Preface

Thanks to him and his talented son, it is less difficult today to journey under the arrangements of the firm to the uttermost parts of the earth than it was 50 years ago to go from London to Edinburgh.

Leicester Chronicle obituary, 23 July 1892.

The name of Thomas Cook is known throughout the world. I have long been intrigued by the life of this remarkable man who was born in humble circumstances and yet was to achieve a position of such international importance and standing. My desire to discover more about the great nineteenth century pioneer has led me to write this book.

A number of biographies have been written about Thomas Cook, notably the two excellent works, *Thomas Cook*, by Piers Brendon and *Thomas Cook of Leicester*, by Robert Ingle, both published in 1991. The purpose of this little book is to focus upon Thomas Cook's local associations during a period of almost 64 years unbroken connection with Leicestershire and Rutland, mainly through his hotel in Granby Street, Leicester.

Thomas Cook's vision and zeal resulted in the opening of the world to tourism. His determination to succeed, together with his deep Baptist faith, his sincerely held temperance beliefs and his benevolent attitude, combine to present a unique and influential personality who made a profound impact upon the world stage.

Derek Seaton
Leicester

Contents

Foreword	i
Preface	ii
Acknowledgements	iv
List of Illustrations	v-vii
A Chronology	viii-x
1 THE FORMATIVE YEARS	1
2 HISTORY IN THE MAKING	18
3 THE TURNING POINT	43
4 FINAL YEARS	65
5 MODERN REMINDERS	101
Appendices	110-116
Family Tree	117
Bibliography	118

Acknowledgements

My sincere thanks are extended to a great many people who have given so generously of their time and knowledge to assist me in the writing of this book.

I acknowledge with gratitude the permission given to reproduce photographs by His Grace the Duke of Rutland CBE, Tim Schadla-Hall, Director of Museums, Arts and Records, Leicestershire County Council, Horace E. Riddington and my good friend Arthur Tomlin.

For permission extended to me to take photographs I am most grateful to His Grace the Duke of Devonshire, John R. Hillier and to the congregations of the Baptist churches at Barton-in-the-Beans, Billesdon and Market Harborough. Also to British Coal (Property Division) for the visit to Coleorton Hall and to the Leicestershire Branch of the British Red Cross Society for the visit to Thorncroft.

For assistance with my research and the use of archive material I am indebted to Steve England and the staff of the Leicester Mercury Library, the staff of the Leicestershire Record Office and with particular thanks to Jill Lomer of Thomas Cook Travel Archive. To the following who provided me with so much valuable information and material to digest, John Faire, Horace Gamble, Mrs Cecily Lankester, Lewis Lowe, Derek Meller, Miss Mavis Mills, John Todd and Douglas Wooldridge. Their assistance was invaluable.

My very sincere thanks go to my friends Ernest Frizelle for the foreword and to Robert Ingle for kindly undertaking the reading of the entire manuscript and for his many helpful suggestions. Finally my thanks to Norman Pilgrim who accompanied me on numerous excursions in the footsteps of Thomas Cook and for the many excellent photographs he produced for inclusion in the book

Illustrations

The Statue of Thomas Cook	Title
All Aboard with Thomas Cook	x
Melbourne, Derbyshire	1
Thomas Cook Close, Melbourne	2
Swarkestone Bridge, Derbyshire	3
The Baptist Chapel, Melbourne	4
Loughborough, Leicestershire	5
The Baptist Church, Billesdon, Leics	6
The Baptist Church, Hinckley, Leics	7
Barton-in-the-Beans, Leics	8
Barrowden, Rutland	9
West Farm, Barrowden, Rutland	10
The Baptist Church, Barrowden	11
Market Harborough, Leics	12
The Parish Church of St Peter, Barrowden	13
Thomas Cook's House in Market Harborough	14
The Baptist Church, Market Harborough	15
William Symington's House and Shop, Market Harborough	16
The Town Hall, Market Harborough	17
The Congregational Church, Kibworth Harcourt, Leics	18
Pillars of Campbell Street Railway Station, Leicester	19
Loughborough Railway Station, Leics	20
William Paget's Park, Southfields, Loughborough	21
The Jewry Wall, Leicester	22
Cramant's Yard, King Street, Leicester	23
The Statue of John Biggs	24
The Methodist Church, Bishop Street, Leicester	25
Mountsorrel, Leics	26
The Baptist Chapel, Barton-in-the-Beans	27
Mount Saint Bernard Abbey, Whitwick, Leics	28
Melbourne Hall, Melbourne	29
William Lamb, Second Viscount Melbourne	30
Belvoir Castle, Leics	31
The Statue of the Fifth Duke of Rutland	32
The Grand Staircase and Landings, Belvoir Castle	33
All Saints Parish Church, Cossington, Leics	34
The Guildhall, Leicester	35
The Museum, New Walk, Leicester	36
Blue Plaque, New Walk Museum	37
The Baptist Church, Charles Street, Leicester	38
Ashby-de-la-Zouch Castle, Leics	39
The Royal Hotel, Ashby-de-la-Zouch	40
Blue Plaque, The Royal Hotel, Ashby-de-la-Zouch	41
Coleorton Hall, Leics	42
Belgrave Hall, Leicester	43

The New Hall, Wellington Street, Leicester	44
Chatsworth House, Derbyshire	45
Paxton's 'Conservative Wall', Chatsworth	46
The Cascade, Chatsworth	47
The Emperor Fountain, Chatsworth	48
Matlock Bath, Derbyshire	49
High Tor, Matlock	50
The Temperance Hotel, Granby Street, Leicester	51
Thornton Reservoir, Leics	52
The Baptist Chapel Graveyard, Melbourne	53
Burghley House, Stamford, Lincs	54
St Martin's Church, Stamford	55
Entrance Gate to St Martin's Churchyard	56
Daniel Lambert's Grave, Stamford	57
The Great Meeting Chapel, Leicester	58
The Corn Exchange, Market Place, Leicester	59
Melbourne Lake	60
St Michael with St. Mary Parish Church, Melbourne	61
The Athenaeum, Melbourne	62
The Temperance Hotel, Leicester	63
Thomas Cook's Rickshaw	64
Thorncroft, London Road, Leicester	65
"Thorncroft"	66
The former Bathroom at Thorncroft	67
The United Baptist Chapel (The Pork Pie Chapel), Leicester	68
The Bust of Annie Elisabeth Cook	69
Eastgates Coffee House, Leicester	70
The High Cross Coffee House, Leicester	71
The Coffee Mills, Springfield Street, Market Harborough	72
The Bookcase presented to Market Harborough Baptist Church	73
The Baptist Chapel, Barton-in-the-Beans	74
The Day School, Barton-in-the-Beans	75
The Deacon Memorial Library, Barton-in-the-Beans	76
Rothesay, Victoria Road, Leicester	77
1 Chancery Street, Leicester	78
The Baptist Memorial Cottages, Melbourne	79
Atlas Chambers, Berridge Street, Leicester	80
102 Regent Road, Leicester	81
Faire Brothers' Factory, Southampton Street, Leicester	82
The Baptist Church, Victoria Road, Leicester	83
Thorncroft, London Road, Leicester	84
The Town Hall, Leicester	85
W.L.Faire's Home, 79 Princess Road, Leicester	86
The Grave of Thomas Cook	87
The Congregational Church, Market Harborough	88

The Home of Thomas Cooper, Churchgate, Leicester	89
The Gladstone Building, Bishop Street, Leicester	90
The Faire Family Vault	91
Inscription on the Faire Family's Monument	92
The Offices of Thomas Cook and Son, Leicester	93
Panel - Leicester to Loughborough 1841	94
Panel - The Great Exhibition 1851	95
Panel - Egypt and the Nile 1884	96
Panel - The Firth of Forth Railway Bridge 1891	97
Nithsdale House, Northampton Road, Market Harborough	98
The grave of John Mason Cook	99
Adderly & Co. Ltd, Market Place, Leicester	100
The Thomas Cook Logo	101
The Plaque at Loughborough Railway Station	102
The Blue Plaque, Thorncroft	103
The Open Book on Thomas Cook's Grave	104
Plaque on the Mission Hall, Melbourne	105
Archdeacon Lane Memorial Baptist Church (ADL), Leicester	106
The 150 Years Commemorative Plaque	107
The Statue of Thomas Cook, London Road, Leicester	108
Robert Ingle (Alias Thomas Cook)	109

APPENDICES

Welford Road Cemetery, Leicester	110
The Reverend Joseph Foulkes Winks	111
John Ellis	112
The Reverend Samuel Wigg	113
Thomas William Hodges	114
John Bennett	115
Henry Lankester	116
Thanksgiving Service	119
A Presentation by Thomas Cook	120

INSIDE REAR COVER
Barton-in-the-Beans Baptist Chapel

REAR COVER
Tom and Bunter

A Chronology of Thomas Cook (1808 - 1892)

1808   Thomas Cook was born at 9 Quick Close, Melbourne, Derbyshire.

1818   At the age of ten Thomas was taken out of school to work for a market gardener.

1822   Apprenticed to his uncle, John Pegg, as a wood-turner and cabinet-maker.

1826   Baptised at Melbourne Baptist Church by the Reverend Joseph Foulkes Winks.

1828   Became a Village Evangelist for the Baptist Missionary Society.

1831   Obliged to leave his missionary work when the Baptist funds diminished.

1832   Moved to Market Harborough to work as a cabinet-maker.

1833   Married Marianne Mason at St Peter's parish church, Barrowden.

1834   Son, John Mason Cook, born at Market Harborough.

1836   Became a total abstainer and helped to form a local Temperance Society.

1841   Organised his first publicly advertised excursion by train from Leicester to Loughborough.

1841   The Cook family moved to No. 1 King Street, Leicester.

1842   As a publisher and printer produced his first *Directory and Guide to Leicester*.

1843   Family moved to No. 26 Granby Street, Leicester.

1844	Expanded his arrangements for Sunday School children to visit parts of Leicestershire and Derbyshire.
1844	Published a new periodical *The National Temperance Magazine*.
1845	Organised his first tourist trips to Liverpool and North Wales.
1845	Daughter, Annie Elizabeth Cook, born in Leicester.
1846	Arranged tours to Scotland via the west coast route.
1848	First organised tours to Belvoir Castle and Chatsworth House.
1851	Responsible for transporting 165,000 people from the Midlands to the Great Exhibition in London.
1853	Cook's *Temperance Hall* and his *Commercial and Family Hotel* opened in Leicester.
1853	Tours of Ireland commenced.
1854	Gave up his printing business and became a full-time Excursion and Tourist Operator.
1855	Organised the first Grand Circular Tour of Europe including a visit to the battlefield of Waterloo.
1861	John Mason Cook married Emma Hodges, of Mayfield, Leicester.
1863	Thomas Cook's first tours of Switzerland followed by Italy in 1864.
1865	First London office opened at No. 98 Fleet Street.
1865	John Mason Cook joined his father and became responsible for the London office.
1866	First tour of America, including visits to the battlefields of the Civil War.

1868   With a party of tourists, attended mark the opening of the railway in his native Melbourne.

1869   Thomas Cook attended the opening of the Suez Canal and arranged his first tour of Palestine, Egypt and the Nile.

1871   John Mason Cook became a partner with his father and the firm became Thomas Cook and Son.

1872   The first "Round the World" tour undertaken by Thomas Cook and nine companions.

1878   Thomas Cook retired. Together with his wife and daughter he went to live at Thorncroft, London Road, Leicester.

1880   Sudden and tragic death of Annie Elizabeth Cook.

1884   Marianne Cook died.

1891   Fourteen Memorial Cottages and a Mission Hall built by Thomas Cook at Melbourne.

1892   Thomas Cook died at Thorncroft, London Road, Leicester, aged 84 years.

All Aboard with Thomas Cook - London Road Railway Station, Leicester, 1995.

1
The Formative Years

Melbourne, Derbyshire

Thomas Cook was born at No. 9 Quick Close, Melbourne, Derbyshire, on 22 November 1808. He was the only son of a poor villager, John Cook, and his wife Elizabeth. His maternal grandfather, Thomas Perkins, came from Hinckley, in Leicestershire and became an influential figure in the New Connexion of General Baptists of which he was one of the founders. The chapels at Barton-in-the-Beans, Leicestershire and Melbourne were major centres of the New Connexion which was founded in 1770.

Thomas Perkins moved to Melbourne in 1760 and became co-preacher with Francis Smith. He was renowned as a preacher of the old 'hell-fire' school and served the Melbourne congregation for 30 years. He died in 1792 when his daughter, Elizabeth, was six years of age.

Thomas Cook Close, Melbourne

The labourer's cottage in which Thomas Cook was born was demolished in 1967. The close, which now bears his name, is situated a few yards away from where the cottage stood.

Elizabeth Cook was the eldest of the three daughters of Thomas Perkins; her sisters were Ann Pegg and Alice Beresford. Thomas Cook's mother could neither read nor write and was able only to make her mark, by means of a cross, in the marriage register. She possessed a deep religious faith and was a devout member of the Baptist congregation.

Thomas Cook was only four years old when his father died in 1812. Later that year his mother married James Smithard who also came from Melbourne.

Swarkestone Bridge, Derbyshire

In 1818, when Thomas Cook was aged ten years, his step-father died. His mother took him out of school and he commenced work for a local market gardener named James Robey for the hard-earned wage of a penny a day. The additional income of sixpence a week was necessary to supplement the family's meagre earnings as there were two young half-brothers, Simeon and James, to feed and clothe.

Young Thomas Cook was required to hawk vegetables and plants around the nearby villages and as far afield as Derby market, a distance of eight miles.

His journeys to Derby took him over Swarkestone Bridge (rebuilt in 1797) with its five impressive arches carrying the main road over the River Trent to the county town.

The Baptist Chapel, Melbourne

During the year 1824, Joseph Foulkes Winks came to Melbourne as the minister of the General Baptist chapel. He had a profound influence on Thomas Cook; it was Winks who baptised the young villager at Melbourne, on 28 February 1826, shortly after his seventeenth birthday.

By this time, the young Thomas Cook had ceased to work for John Robey and had commenced an apprenticeship, as a wood-turner and cabinet-maker, with his uncle, John Pegg, in Melbourne. Each of these early employers was to leave a lasting impression on their teen-age worker as both were heavy drinkers and Thomas witnessed that they were often inebriated and incapable of carrying out their work.

Loughborough, Leicestershire

Joseph Winks remained at Melbourne for only two years. He moved to Loughborough in late 1826 where he set up a printing press and became a publisher to the General Baptist Association.

* Thomas Cook followed Winks to Loughborough in 1827 and remained with him for a short time during which he learned the rudiments of the printing trade. This was to prove invaluable to him in later years.

In 1830, Joseph Winks went to live in Leicester where he established himself once again, in High Street, as a printer and publisher. He was responsible for a range of Baptist publications and personally edited five monthly magazines.

The Baptist Church, Billesdon, Leicestershire

In October 1828, shortly before his twentieth birthday, having returned to his native Melbourne, Thomas Cook was appointed an evangelist by the Village Missionary Society of the Baptist church. His task, for which he was initially paid £36 per annum, was to preach the Word, distribute pamphlets and establish Sunday schools.

In 1888, he recorded: "I began my visits at Billesdon in 1829 where Mr Creaton was then labouring in the double capacity of minister and schoolmaster".

The Billesdon Baptist church opened for worship on 19 April 1813. William Henry Creaton was the second pastor and served from 1816 to 1837. He established a boarding school for boys in a three story house by the side of the church and was both pastor and the principal of the school which was known as The Academy.

The Baptist Church, Hinckley, Leicestershire

Thomas Cook held meetings at Hinckley in 1829, where the Reverend James Taylor was pastor from 1822-1845. He was to record, on a later visit to Hinckley, that James Taylor advised him: "By all means to get home as soon as possible, as he had the impression that I should not be long-lived if I continued in that work".

The visits to Hinckley enabled Thomas Cook to return to his roots since it was the former home of his grandfather, Thomas Perkins.

The building of the Hinckley Baptist church commenced in March 1806. The cost of the work was almost £1800 and the opening took place on 18 February 1807 with a sermon delivered by the great Baptist preacher, the Reverend Robert Hall, who was minister at Harvey Lane Baptist church, in Leicester, from 1807 to 1825.

Barton-in-the-Beans, Leicestershire

Thomas Cook's travels as an evangelist also took him to Barton where he recorded: "It was my privilege to make the acquaintance of the Reverend John Derry and to hold a meeting in the General Baptist chapel". John Derry was pastor of the Barton chapel for 28 years (1824-1852). Thomas Cook went on to visit Barlestone, Nailstone, Market Bosworth, Hugglescote, Ibstock and Measham, in Leicestershire.

The quaintly named hamlet of Barton-in-the-Beans, in the west of the county, is associated with the rich bean-growing area of Leicestershire where the crops formed part of the staple diet of the medieval yeomen. Generations of county school children soon learned the answer to, "how many beans make five?".

Barrowden, Rutland

Thomas Cook reflected upon his journeys as a young missionary and wrote: "These long tours gave me a very interesting insight into the combinations and working arrangements of the General Baptist Churches, which added much to my interest in the prosperity of the Denomination and gave me many very pleasant interviews with the Ministers of that period".

Eventually, following extensive tours of Leicestershire and visits to Derbyshire and Nottingham, Thomas Cook returned to the village of Barrowden, in Rutland, where he was originally based when he commenced his missionary activities in 1828.

He continued to tour the villages and he recorded that in the year 1829, he covered 2692 miles of which 2106 were actually walked.

The Farmhouse, West Farm, Barrowden, Rutland

During 1829, Thomas Cook met Marianne Mason, the twenty-one year old daughter of a Barrowden farmer, Henry Mason. The Mason family lived at West Farm where Marianne cared for her father and five brothers following the death of her mother when Marianne was a young girl.

Henry Mason is shown in *White's Directory of Leicestershire* for 1846 as being a farmer, grazier and maltster. The farmhouse is dated 1724 and is built of local limestone and ironstone.

Marianne Mason was a very resourceful young lady, a good housekeeper and a little mother to her five brothers. She and Thomas fell in love and their courtship was to last for four years.

The Baptist Church, Barrowden

Marianne Mason was a teacher at the Baptist Sunday School and shared the same strength of conviction in her nonconformist faith as did Thomas. The limestone chapel, where she taught, was built in 1819.

In 1831, the funds of the Baptist Missionary Society could no longer support the work of the village missionaries and it was no longer possible for Thomas Cook to earn a living in that way.

He switched to wood-turning and cabinet-making, but the tiny village of Barrowden could not support him in a full-time occupation and he was forced to consider a move to a town of some size.

Market Harborough, Leicestershire
(The Free Grammar School was built in 1814 by Robert Smyth)

In 1832, Thomas Cook moved to Market Harborough where he again set up as a wood-turner.

The population of the town was then just under 2500; a small busy market town where the chief trade was an extensive manufacturing of carpets and worsteds by the firm of Messrs John Clarke & Sons; there were six straw hat makers and the number of inns, hotels, taverns and public houses totalled twenty-four.

The Royal Mail coach from Manchester to London called daily, at 9.30pm, at the Three Swans in High Street.

The Parish Church of Saint Peter, Barrowden

Thomas Cook and Marianne Mason were married on 2 March 1833 by the Rector of Barrowden, the Reverend Richard Carey, at St Peter's church, in Marianne's home village. Richard Carey was rector of the early 13th century church for 45 years, from 1795 to 1840.

At that time, marriage was not possible in nonconformist chapels and remained so until the passing of the Marriage Act in 1837.

Thomas Cook's House in Market Harborough

Thomas and his bride set up home in Market Harborough, in quaintly named Adam and Eve Street. Their first child, John Mason Cook, was born on Plough Monday, 13 January 1834. A second son, Henry, was born in August 1835, but survived only four weeks.

Thomas Cook was described in *Pigot and Company's Director for Leicestershire* (1835) as being, "a wood and brass turner, toyman and Windsor chair maker".

The Baptist Church, Coventry Road, Market Harborough

Whilst in Market Harborough, Thomas Cook became a member of the small Baptist church which had been built in 14 weeks from the laying of the foundation stone on 8 March to the opening on 17 July 1831.

The Reverend Francis Beardsall was the minister from 1832 to 1834 and, as the local agent of the British and Foreign Temperance Society, he was to exert a profound influence on the young wood-turner and his wife. Under his guidance, Thomas Cook signed the temperance pledge in January 1833 and Marianne signed four months later. The pledge required that spirits should not be consumed - wine and beer were permissible in moderation.

William Symington's House and Shop in High Street Market Harborough

In 1836, Thomas Cook became a total abstainer. The first local Temperance Society was formed in January 1836 when a group of seven people signed the pledge in William Symington's drawing room. Thomas became the first secretary and William the first president.

William Symington came from his native Lanarkshire in 1827 and set himself up as a tea and coffee merchant.

The Town Hall, High Street, Market Harborough
(Built by the Earl of Harborough in 1788)

Many of the early temperance meetings were held in the Town Hall. The temperance workers frequently met with verbal abuse and their meetings disrupted. Those who spoke out against what they saw as the social evils of heavy drinking were subjected to attacks of violence by street mobs; the windows of their homes were smashed, including those of Thomas and Marianne Cook.

On one occasion, Thomas Cook was knocked to the ground by a legbone of a horse which was thrown at him by an anti-teetotal protester. He managed to get to his feet and chased and apprehended his attacker who was duly charged with physical assault.

2
History in the making

*The Congregational Church, Kibworth Harcourt
Leicestershire - built 1761*

On 9 June 1841, Thomas Cook set out to walk from Market Harborough to Leicester, a distance of 15 miles, to attend a Temperance Society meeting in the town. Shortly after passing the Congregational chapel and parsonage in Kibworth Harcourt, an idea occurred to him. In his words: "A thought flashed through my brain - what a glorious thing it would be if the newly developed powers of railways and locomotion could be made subservient to the promotion of temperance".

He suggested to the meeting that he should be authorised to hire a train and carriages to transport the Leicester members to the quarterly meeting of delegates to be held at Loughborough the following month. He received the enthusiastic support of the meeting.

The Twin Pillars of the Entrance to the former Railway Station in Campbell Street, Leicester.

Monday the fifth of July 1841 was the day on which the first railway excursion, arranged by Thomas Cook, left Leicester for Loughborough. The *Leicester Chronicle* of the 10th reported that the train, hired from the Midland Counties Railway Company, "was put on to convey the whole party to and from Loughborough at the low charge of one shilling per passenger". There were some 485 passengers including John Mason Cook, then aged seven years, who accompanied his father on the epic journey.

A huge crowd witnessed the departure of the train from Leicester and many gathered at the bridges *en route* to view the party travelling in open tub-type carriages. They were accompanied on board by, "an excellent band and were headed by their district officers and flags".

Loughborough Railway Station
(The lower section of the present platform is what remains of the platform of 1841)

Thomas Cook's Temperance Excursion duly arrived at Loughborough and was greeted by a large and excited crowd of onlookers.

The Leicester Temperance members were joined in the town by fellow members from Derby and Nottingham. They marched together through Loughborough and the *Leicester Chronicle* reported: "they perambulated the town in good array - the whole population lining the streets and filling the windows as they passed by". The party was accompanied by the band and when they reached the market place they halted, formed themselves into a circle and "sang the Teetotal National Anthem".

William Paget's Park, Southfields, Loughborough

The Temperance party was, "most cordially welcomed" by William Paget outside his house at Southfields where he received the leaders of the procession whilst the band played the National Anthem.

Tea was taken at the park and was followed by games such as 'kiss in the ring', 'running under the handkerchief' and 'tag'. Others played cricket. By early evening, almost 3000 people had assembled and the rest of the time was taken up with speeches by temperance leaders on the social evils of drinking and the benefits of temperance.

The party arrived back on the platform of Leicester station at 10.30pm: "the rest", as they say, "is history".

The Jewry Wall, St Nicholas Circle, Leicester
(The ruins of part of a complex of Roman buildings)

In September 1841, two months after Thomas Cook's first excursion to Loughborough, the family moved to Leicester.

Their first home in the town was at No.1 King Street and Thomas commenced his business as bookseller and stationer whilst continuing to devote his energies to the work of the Temperance movement.

The population of Leicester in 1841 was recorded as 48,167. Some 3497 were employed in the long-established hosiery industry and 660 men and women earned a living in the manufacture of boots and shoes, a comparatively new industry in Leicester at that time.

The town was a very unhealthy place in which to live: wells, but no reservoir supply, a polluted River Soar and a life expectancy of 25 years.

Cramant's Yard, King Street, Leicester

Working class housing in Leicester in the 1840s often consisted of hastily erected tiny cottages tightly grouped together in courts and yards.

The Cook family initially resided in an area of the town close to where many poor families lived in overcrowded dwellings lacking basic amenities. The only existing example of such housing from that period is to be found in Cramant's yard which was built in the 1820s. This row of cottages, situated close to Thomas Cook's home, comprised six one-up, one-down, back-to-back houses where people huddled together for warmth and shelter.

The census of 1841 recorded 22 people living in Cramant cottages; the cottages underwent a major restoration in the late 1980s.

The Statue of John Biggs (1801-1871)
Welford Place, Leicester

During 1841, a new warehouse was opened in Belvoir Street, Leicester, by John and William Biggs, the town's largest hosiery manufacturers. John Biggs, a Unitarian and a man with a social conscience, placed the warehouse at the disposal of the Leicester Temperance Society. In the words of Thomas Cook, it was used for, "a great tea meeting which comprehended 1000 guests".

The Methodist Church, Bishop Street, Leicester

In 1842, Thomas Cook introduced his *Leicestershire Almanack, Directory, Guide to Leicester and Advertiser.* He compiled and published his little book at No.1 King Street and made it available for sale through booksellers in the county.

The guide was well received and drew a great deal of admiration. It contained 170 pages of detailed information relating to the town and was sold for one shilling - in a wrapper.

All the churches and "dissenting chapels" were listed, including Bishop Street Wesleyan Methodist church which was built by the Reverend William Jenkins in 1815. Cook recorded that services were held there at 10.30am and 6.00pm on Sundays and at 7.00pm on weekdays. The minister was the Reverend H. Powis and the chapel was noted as being "licensed for the Celebration of Marriage".

Mountsorrel, Leicestershire
(The 1793 Butter Market of William Thomas)

By the year 1844, Thomas Cook had successfully organised a large number of Sunday school outings and in the previous year had arranged for 3000 children from Leicester to visit Derbyshire. The outings took place during Race Week in Leicester, which was held in September and timed to keep the children "away from temptation".

In the same year, he arranged for a similar party on a local outing. He was assisted by his ten-year old son, John, who later described the event thus: "My public career as a Personal Conductor commenced in 1844 as a small boy with a long wand assisting the guidance of 500 other children from Leicester to Syston by special train - five miles; then a two mile walk across fields to Mountsorrel Hills for an afternoon's picnic and back the same route to Leicester".

The Baptist Chapel, Barton-in-the-Beans

The centenary celebrations to mark the building of Barton's first chapel in 1745 were held in the hamlet on 15 May 1845. About 800 people attended. The present chapel was erected in 1841 on the site of the original building.

Thomas Cook compiled and produced a commemorative publication, *The Barton Centenary*, on 19 June 1845, in which he noted the following: Members 352; Sabbath School 351; Teachers 42. (Extracted from the 1844 tabular list of Baptist churches)

In the preface to the book he wrote: "That the blessing of Him who has so smiled on this part of his vineyard, may attend the publication of these memoirs is the fervent prayer of the compiler".

Mount Saint Bernard Abbey, Whitwick, Leicestershire

August 1848 saw Thomas Cook making a return visit to his native Melbourne in some style. He arranged for a party of 109 people to make the journey from Leicester in nine horse-drawn carriages. En route to Melbourne, the party called at Mount St Bernard Abbey, situated in the rugged and beautiful Charnwood Forest area.

The actual visit to the Abbey took place only after negotiations upon arrival: whilst the men in the party were allowed entrance, the women were excluded.

Mount St Bernard Abbey was built as a monastery by Augustus Welby Pugin in 1844 and became an abbey in 1848. It was the first in England since the Reformation. In the 1840s, the monks fed tens of thousands of desperately poor people each year, many of whom they provided with lodgings.

Melbourne Hall, Melbourne, Derbyshire

The party of excursionists reached Thomas Cook's beloved Melbourne shortly after mid-day. They were given a rousing welcome by large crowds of villagers accompanied by a brass band. The afternoon was spent touring the grounds of the hall which were laid out in 1704 by the Right Honourable Thomas Coke (1675-1727). Tea was taken at a nearby school before the return journey to Leicester in the late afternoon.

Melbourne Hall, as viewed by Cook and his party, was substantially altered by Sir John Coke (1563-1644) in the seventeenth century. The hall, which underwent a number of alterations and significant extensions through the centuries, must have appeared a very palatial and splendid building to many of the party travelling out of Leicestershire for the first time in their lives.

William Lamb, Second Viscount Melbourne

The visit to Melbourne Hall also enabled Thomas Cook's excursionists to reflect upon the great Victorian statesman, William Lamb (1779-1848) who owned the hall from 1828 until his death. William Lamb succeeded to the title and inherited the family estates upon the death of his father in July 1828.

William Lamb left the legal profession and entered politics as Member of Parliament for Leominster in 1805. In June 1834 he became Prime Minister, but held office for a brief period of only five months. He again became Prime Minister in 1835 and remained in office until May 1841.

During Lord Melbourne's second term, the Bearbrass settlement, in Victoria, Australia, was renamed in his honour. More importantly, Queen Victoria came to the throne on 20 June 1837 and was to rely heavily upon him for guidance and support which he gave unstintingly to the young Queen.

Belvoir Castle, the Leicestershire Home of the Dukes of Rutland

On 29 August 1848, Thomas Cook conducted "A Pleasure Party" from Leicester, again by horse-drawn carriages, to Belvoir Castle. He provided the visitors with a *Handbook of Belvoir Castle* which he had compiled and which he sold at threepence a copy. The handbook gave a detailed description of the castle and grounds, together with information about the villages in the Vale of Belvoir. He also included hints on, "how to behave in the castle and grounds".

Refreshments were available at the nearby Belvoir Inn which was described in the handbook in the following terms: "While the accommodation is suitable for visitors of first rank, we believe that the humbler classes are supplied with refreshments on economical terms thus superseding the necessity for numerous basket accompaniments and annoyance of pic-nic parties".

John Henry Manners, 5th Duke of Rutland (1778-1857)

Arrangements for the visit to Belvoir Castle were made between Thomas Cook and the Duke of Rutland. In his handbook, Thomas commented: "We understand that it is the wish of the noble proprietor of the Castle that all should have free access, providing they behave with propriety and decorum". The visitors were shown round in parties of twenty-five.

The statue of the fifth Duke, which stands in Leicester Market Place, was erected in 1852 to commemorate the Golden Jubilee of his service as Lord Lieutenant of Leicestershire.

The Grand Staircase and Landings, Belvoir Castle
(By kind permission of His Grace, the Duke of Rutland)

The history of Belvoir Castle dates back to the late 11th century. In 1816, parts of the castle were severely damaged by a fire which resulted in the redesigning of the exterior and the damaged wings. The work was completed in 1830.

Both the Duke and Thomas Cook were pleased with the outcome of the first visit in 1848 and further visits were arranged.

All Saints Parish Church, Cossington, Leicestershire

On 21 September 1848, a Rural Festival was held at Cossington to commemorate the anniversary of the Leicester Temperance Society which had been founded 12 years earlier.

Thomas Cook had first visited the village with a party of temperance workers in 1839. The later excursion was by means of a special train consisting of 48 carriages which conveyed a large party of members. The event was recorded in the *Leicester Chronicle* of 23 September which reported that, "upwards of 1500 of the members and friends made the seven mile journey to Cossington Gate".

The 13th century church was crowded to hear the Rector, the Reverend John Babington, then President of of the Society, preach the sermon. The *Leicester Chronicle* report concluded: "tea was served on the gravel walk, beneath an extensive grove, adjoining the rectory, upon a table 126 yards long".

The Guildhall, Guildhall Lane, Leicester
(Served as Leicester's Town Hall from 1563 to 1876)

In the 1840s, the Leicester Temperance Society was unrelenting in its fight against the social evils and misery caused by drinking. The passing of the Beerhouse Act in 1830, designed to offset the drinking of spirits, resulted in 44,000 new beerhouses being opened within the space of six years. In Leicester alone there were 242 hotels, inns and taverns plus 129 beerhouses (*White's Directory of Leicestershire*, 1846).

Thomas Cook recorded in 1849: "More than 2000 members have been enrolled in the abstinence pledge book, regular meetings are held on Tuesday and Saturday evenings in the Town Hall". Plans were in hand for the building of a temperance hall capable of seating 1665 when Thomas Cook was joint secretary of the Leicester Society.

The 14th century Guildhall was built by the Guild of Corpus Christi and is now a Grade 1 Listed Building.

The New Walk Museum, Leicester

In 1849, Thomas Cook compiled, printed and published his last *Annual Guide to Leicester*. He described many of Leicester's buildings and the services they offered in considerable detail. One such building was the Town Museum in New Walk.

The building, which stands in Leicester's unique walkway, laid out in 1785, contained an important collection of exhibits. Thomas Cook's description read as follows:

> *This museum collection was commenced by the Literary and Philosophical Society and was presented to the Corporation for the benefit of the Town in 1846. It is a great attraction and ornament and when the arrangement of the collection is completed will be an instructive lounge for the lovers of science. The Literary and Philosophical Society have meetings every other Monday evening to hear papers read upon literary and scientific subjects.*

The New Walk museum is now the responsibility of the Leicestershire Museums, Arts and Records Service.

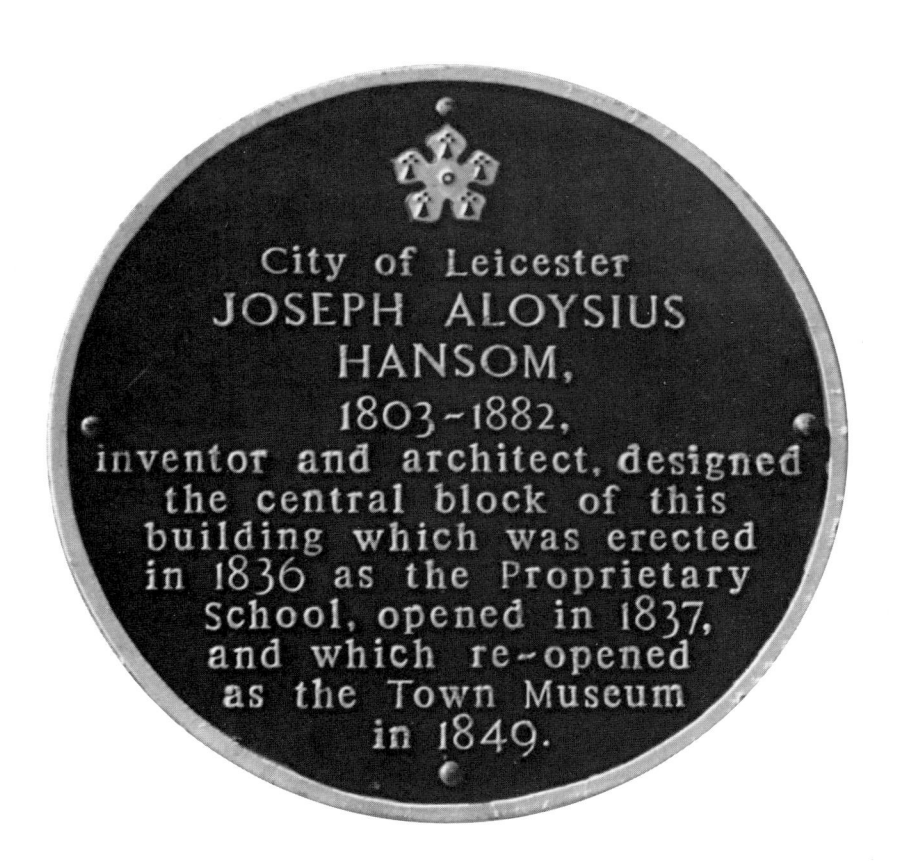

> City of Leicester
> JOSEPH ALOYSIUS HANSOM,
> 1803-1882,
> inventor and architect, designed the central block of this building which was erected in 1836 as the Proprietary School, opened in 1837, and which re-opened as the Town Museum in 1849.

The Blue Plaque on the Front of the New Walk Museum

The plaque records that the building was originally designed by Joseph Aloysius Hansom as a Proprietary School and was opened in 1837. It provided a private education for the sons of nonconformist families and it possessed a number of exceptionally talented masters on the staff. The school experienced severe financial difficulties and was closed in 1847.

Joseph Hansom, a native of York, resided in Hinckley from 1834 to 1841 during which time he invented the Hansom cab.

The former school was officially opened as the town's first museum on 19 June 1849, by the Mayor, William Biggs.

The Baptist Church, Charles Street,
(William Flint - 1831)

In his last *Guide to Leicester* (price one shilling) which Thomas Cook printed at his small shop at No. 1 Campbell Street, Leicester, he included detailed information on the churches and chapels in the town.

His description of William Flint's building read:

> *Charles Street Chapel is a neat edifice erected for the accommodation of the Second Particular Baptist Church. It will seat about 700 people. The congregation includes several very influential families and the senior Member of Parliament of the Borough (Richard Harris) is an officebearer in the Church. The Sunday School contains about 260 scholars and 26 teachers. Services on Sunday: 10.30am and 6.30pm and a lecture on Thursday Evening at 6.30pm.*

The Ruins of Ashby-de-la-Zouch Castle, Leicestershire

On 1 June 1850, Thomas Cook arranged "A Grand Pic-Nic Day" at Ashby-de-la-Zouch in north-west Leicestershire. A special train was advertised with first class carriage fare at three shillings and six pence (17½p.) return and covered carriage at two shillings (10p.) return. This was the first pleasure trip to Ashby since the opening of the railway there in 1849 and arrangements were made for the people of the town to be involved. Thomas Cook stated on his handbills for the trip: "It is expected that business will be generally suspended and every facility will be given for viewing the various places and objects of interest in the Town".

The building of Ashby Castle was commenced by the Beaumonts, earls of Leicester from 1150 onwards. William, Lord Hastings, became the owner and in 1474 obtained authority to build the imposing tower which was to bear his name. He was executed by order of King Richard III in 1483.

The Royal Hotel, Ashby-de-la-Zouch, Leicestershire

The outing to Ashby included visits to the Ivanhoe Baths, the Royal Hotel and the Pleasure Grounds. A 'cold collation' was available at the hotel between 12.00 noon and 2.00pm at a shilling per head for the visitors.

Popular amusements were arranged at the Pleasure Grounds and two "Powerful Brass Bands" were engaged. One band was provided by Henry Nicholson (1825-1907), the nationally renowned flautist and conductor, a native of Leicester; the other was the Melbourne Band from Thomas Cook's nearby birthplace.

The Royal Hotel, formerly the Hastings Hotel, was built by Robert Chaplin in 1826-7; his design incorporated the large porch with its dual pairs of Greek Doric stone columns.

*The Blue Plaque on the Royal Hotel
Ashby-de-la-Zouch*

The plaque, on the right of the front entrance to the Royal Hotel, links the building with the 1822 Ivanhoe Baths of Robert Chaplin. Originally, water for the baths was transported, by canal, from Moira where the Hastings family, who owned the local coal-mine, had discovered remedial waters in the mine.

Thomas Cook's visitors had the opportunity to sample the waters, "at the reduced rate of 6d. for a warm fresh water bath and the salt water baths at very reduced rates".

The Ivanhoe Baths were closed in the 1880s and demolished in 1962.

Coleorton Hall, Coleorton, Leicestershire

An added attraction during the visit to Ashby-de-la-Zouch was the opportunity to visit Coleorton Hall. Thomas Cook arranged with the Royal Hotel and local 'Coach Proprietors' to convey members of the party to Coleorton, a distance of two miles, at a nominal charge of sixpence each.

He had obtained the permission of the hall's owner, Sir George Beaumont Bart, for the excursionists to view the beautiful Winter and Italian Gardens which were designed by the romantic poet, William Wordsworth, in 1806. In his handbills, Thomas Cook declared: "Visitors will be conducted through the grounds by Mr Henderson the head gardener. Visitors are requested not to pluck the flowers or handle the statues".

Coleorton Hall was demolished by the forces of Oliver Cromwell in the Civil War and rebuilt by Sir George Beaumont, a great patron of the arts.

3
The Turning Point

Belgrave Hall, Church Road, Belgrave, Leicester
(Built 1709-13 - it is now the Belgrave Hall Museum)

By 1850, Thomas Cook was beginning to think of arranging a trip to America, but his dream was not to be realised for some years to come. It was whilst he was on his way to Liverpool to discuss shipping arrangements that he met John Ellis and John Paxton in Derby.

John Ellis was chairman of the Midland Railway Company and lived at Belgrave Hall on the outskirts of Leicester. He had been influential in securing the services of Robert Stephenson to build the Leicester to Swannington railway in 1832 - the third railway to be opened in Britain. Ellis and Paxton, who was head gardener to the Duke of Devonshire at Chatsworth, persuaded Cook to concentrate all his energies upon arranging the transportation by rail of people from the Midlands to the Great Exhibition in Hyde Park, London, in 1851. Cook agreed and began to embark upon his next great challenge.

The New Hall, Wellington Street, Leicester (1832 - Wm Flint)
(Now the Leicestershire Central Lending Library)

On 21 January 1851, Thomas Cook arranged a meeting at the New Hall to which he invited the townspeople to learn of his plans to convey visitors to the Great Exhibition. He also explained that he had arranged lodgings in London for working men attending the exhibition, "at one shilling per night, breakfast including meat for 9d. per head". The advertisement stated, "no gambling, quarrelling, fighting, profane or abusive language to be allowed".

The exhibition proved to be a turning point in the great excursionist's career: it is recorded that he arranged for 165,000 people to travel and to participate in this momentous event in British history.

Thomas Cook was very fond of the New Hall where he often spoke on the subject of temperance. He wrote in 1849: "This excellent institution (used by the Mechanics Institute) has a library of some 2950 volumes the issues from which last year were 13,030".

Chatsworth House, Derbyshire

In May 1851 Thomas Cook, whilst busily involved in the final arrangements for the Great Exhibition, organised excursions by train to Chatsworth and Matlock. Initially he had taken a party to Chatsworth in 1848 and was entranced by the beauty of his native county.

On 31 March he had published the first edition of *Cook's Exhibition and Excursion Advertiser* in which he described Chatsworth in considerable detail. The building of the great house commenced in 1552 and became the home of the Cavendish family - the Dukes of Devonshire.

Thomas Cook spoke of Chatsworth in the following terms: "Chatsworth is perhaps on the whole the most splendid residence in England and well deserves its title of the Palace of the Peak".

The Central Section of Paxton's 'Conservative Wall'

Thomas Cook had great admiration for the work and achievements of Joseph Paxton (1801-65). He marvelled at Paxton's skill and creativeness in iron and glass. The excursionists to Chatsworth were able to see the 'Conservative Wall' which Paxton had completed in 1848. It was designed as a series of steps taking the conservatory up a hillside, a distance of 331 feet.

His visitors also saw the Great Conservatory, completed by Paxton in 1840. In his *Excursion Advertiser,* Cook described it as, "The largest in the world - being 300 feet in length and 145 feet in width with a central arch which was 65 feet high". The Great Conservatory, as Cook explained, "was the original idea of the Crystal Palace" designed by Paxton for the Great Exhibition of 1851. The Great Conservatory was demolished in 1920.

The Cascade, Chatsworth Garden

The visitors from Leicester were able also to admire the beauty of The Cascade - an impressive series of 24 sets of paving stones bringing the water down a slope from the Cascade House to an underground piped system feeding two of the fountains in the grounds of Chatsworth. The Cascade was laid out in 1696 and considerably extended in the early part of the 18th century.

The excursions to Chatsworth were extremely popular and Thomas Cook established a good relationship with the sixth Duke of Devonshire (1790-1858) who agreed to the parties visiting Chatsworth from 1848 onwards.

Cook described the Chatsworth estate as being, "Fourteen miles in circumference with its 2000 head of deer and the beautiful gardens and grounds surrounding the house of Mr Paxton".

The Emperor Fountain, Chatsworth

Joseph Paxton was extremely gifted in the laying out of gardens and the creation of fountains. The Emperor Fountain, by Paxton, was completed in 1844 and was named, by the Sixth Duke, after Czar Nicholas I, Emperor of Russia. It is recorded that the fountain reached a height of 296 feet. Paxton was knighted in 1851.

Matlock Bath, Derbyshire

The 1851 railway excursion to Derbyshire enabled those visitors who wished, to leave the train at Matlock Bath station and spend the day in the town, or by the River Derwent and the surrounding area, before rejoining the train in the evening.

Thomas Cook, in his *Excursion Advertiser* had this to say about the popular spa town: "Matlock too has charms with which no other part of England can vie. Its singularly interesting caverns, lofty eminences, beautiful slopes and terraces, minerals and petrifications and the production products of its artists, render it a place of attraction from which the visitor is never weary".

High Tor, Matlock

An outstanding feature of the visits to Matlock was the sight of High Tor, a 350 foot vertical wall of limestone rock overlooking the valley of the Derwent.

Thomas Cook said in 1851, "Again and again have Midlanders visited this delightful district and still a trip to Matlock and Chatsworth is always popular".

He produced, in meticulous detail, descriptions of the various venues he had to offer to his excursionists. An example of his distinctive advertising style is to be found in the first number of his *Cook's Exhibition Herald and Excursion Advertiser* for 31 May 1851: Every visitor should possess a copy of next week's *Excursion Herald* which will be devoted principally to the description of the neighbourhood and will be the cheapest Guide to this part of Derbyshire ever produced".

The Temperance Hotel, Granby Street, Leicester

During 1853, Thomas Cook realised two further ambitions. The year saw the opening of his Commercial & Family Temperance Hotel and the Temperance Hall, in Granby Street, Leicester. The properties were contiguous, but their immediate neighbours, either side, were The Nag's Head and The Wagon and Horses !

Thornton Reservoir, Leicestershire

On 21 December 1853, Thomas Cook's Temperance Hall became the first building in Leicester to receive piped water from the newly constructed Thornton reservoir. It was perhaps appropriate for the ardent temperance supporter to be able to accept the first supply of fresh water and he must have considered it a wonderful gift to receive for Christmas. The ceremony to mark the occasion was attended by the Mayor of the Borough, Alderman Samuel How, a Leicester hosiery manufacturer.

The Temperance Hall became the Cinema-de-Luxe in 1916, the Princess Cinema in 1929 and finally, the Essoldo Cinema in the l950s. The building was demolished in 1961.

The Baptist Chapel Graveyard, Melbourne

Thomas Cook's mother, Mrs Elizabeth Tivey (she had married for a third time), died 23 February 1854, aged 66 years. Her gifted son wrote of her in 1890: "James Smithard, (his stepfather) died at Melbourne in 1818 and after his burial my mother took me into her bedroom and laying her hands on my head said now Tommy you must be father to these two boys" (his halfbrothers, James and Simeon). Times had been desperately hard for the young Thomas Cook and his mother, but their deep Baptist faith sustained them through their struggles.

Elizabeth Tivey was buried in her native Melbourne. Thomas, when writing about his parents, recalled: "John Cook my father died in 1812 and was buried in the chapel graveyard but no stone was erected to perpetuate his memory and my mother, who died in 1854, was interred as near as possible to his resting place".

Burghley House, Stamford, Lincolnshire

In 1857 and again in 1858, Thomas Cook arranged railway excursions to Stamford and Burghley House; 1857 was the year in which the Marquis of Exeter gave his consent for excursion parties to visit Burghley House for the first time.

In the *Leicester Chronicle* of 25 April 1857, Thomas Cook referred to Burghley House as, "that noble Elizabethan Palace". The great house was built between 1565 and 1587 by William Cecil Burghley, the First Baron (1520-98), chief adviser to Queen Elizabeth I, Lord High Treasurer of England and a distinguished 16th century statesman.

A handbill, printed by Cook, described Burghley as: "The celebrated park and princely mansion of the Most Noble, the Marquis of Exeter, K.G.". He recorded after the visit, "a large party of Ladies, Gentlemen and Pupils paid one shilling each for admission".

Saint Martin's Church, Stamford

Thomas Cook's day trip to Stamford on Monday, 7 June 1858, was described as a visit to: "The ancient and interesting town of Stamford". He arranged for all the churches in the town to be open, "to the inspection of visitors, in one of them - St. Martin's - there are five monuments to the great Lord Burghley and others of the Cecil Family".

The beautiful parish church of St Martin's stands in the southern part of Stamford and is thought to have been built between 1480 and 1485. William Cecil, Lord Burghley, is commemorated in the form of a magnificent monument in marble and alabaster which is an outstanding example of such work from the Renaissance period.

The church also contains an effigy of his parents, Richard Cecil (died 1522) and his wife Jane (died 1587). There are some fine 15th century stained glass windows which the excursionists would have been able to admire, together with the work of 1844 when the seating was renewed in oak and a new pulpit and reading desk installed.

The Entrance to Saint Martin's Churchyard, Stamford

In his publicity for the visit to Stamford and Burghley, Thomas Cook referred to, "The Leicester prodigy of 52 stones Daniel Lambert who died in Stamford and his Grave Head Stone may be seen".

Daniel Lambert was born on 13 March 1770, in Blue Boar Lane, Leicester. In 1791, he succeeded his father as keeper of the County Bridewell in the town. His weight began to increase dramatically in his early twenties and by the time he was twenty-three, he weighed over 30 stone. It became necessary for him to leave his employment as a gaoler in 1804 - his weight grew and eventually he reached 52 stone and 11 pounds (335kg).

In June 1809, Lambert arrived in Stamford on a tour which had included Cambridge and Huntingdon. He had visited Stamford to attend the races, but collapsed and died in the Waggon and Horses Inn, on 21 June.

Daniel Lambert's Grave, Saint Martin's Churchyard, Stamford

The headstone, in Swithland slate, records that Daniel Lambert, "was possessed of an excellent and convivial Mind and in personal Greatness had no Competitor. As a testimony of Respect this stone is erected by his Friends in Leicester".

The Great Meeting, Unitarian Chapel, East Bond Street, Leicester

Christmas 1861 was the occasion of a wedding in the Cook family. On 27 December, John Mason Cook married Emma Hodges, eldest daughter of Thomas William Hodges, elastic web manufacturer, of Mayfield, Stoneygate, Leicester. They were married at the Great Meeting by the Reverend Charles C. Coe who was minister there for 20 years (1855-74). Built in 1708, the Great Meeting was one of the first brick buildings in Leicester.

John Mason and Emma Cook set up their first home in Sparkenhoe Street, Leicester, literally in the shadow of the town's Union Workhouse which was built in 1838, Their first child, a son, whom they named Frank Henry, was born on 25 September 1862. John Mason Cook's occupation was shown on the birth certificate as corn dealer.

The Corn Exchange, Market Place, Leicester

One winter's evening in February 1866, Thomas Cook gave a lecture in Leicester's Corn Exchange. the *Leicester Journal* of 28 February reported: "The large audience was held spellbound by the lecturer's vivid account of his recent reconnaissance trip to America prior to his leading the first ever tour of the United States". Thomas Cook's voyage across the Atlantic took 11 days 12 hours and during the next two weeks of his stay, he covered some 4000 miles.

Melbourne Lake

On 10 September 1868, a "Special Express Train" left Leicester at 2.30pm bound for Melbourne. The half-day excursion had been arranged by Thomas Cook to celebrate the opening of the new railway line connecting Derby with Melbourne. The Midland Railway Company poster advertising the event, declared,
"Melbourne being the native place of the Agent for Midland Railway Excursions, he was anxious to have the privilege of arranging the First Excursion to that town".

Thomas Cook accompanied the party, having organised a full afternoon's activities which included a visit to Melbourne Hall gardens by permission of Lady Palmerston, also the parks and grounds surrounding Melbourne lake which was described in the advertisement as, "A sheet of water covering about 20 acres with two beautiful islands - accessible by boat".

*Saint Michael with Saint Mary Parish Church
Melbourne*

A visit to the magnificent 12th century parish church was arranged as part of the itinerary for the Melbourne excursion. The excusionists marvelled at the beauty of one of the finest examples of Norman church architecture to be found in a village setting. For Thomas Cook the church had emotional associations for it was there that his parents, John Cook and Elizabeth Perkins, were married in February 1808.

The Athenaeum, Potter Street, Melbourne
(Now part of the Methodist church buildings)

An important building visited by Thomas Cook and his party was the Athenaeum, the foundation stone of which was laid by Lord Palmerston. It was built in 1853 at a cost of £1200 and contained a library, an infants' school, a mechanics institute and a savings bank.

Tea was arranged at the Athenaeum for a hundred visitors at a shilling a head. Those not included had tea at the Melbourne Arms where cold meat and eggs were provided at one shilling and threepence per person.

In the evening. Thomas Cook gave a lecture in the Athenaeum. Admission was free and he addressed the inhabitants and visitors on, "My Excursion and Tourist life since leaving Melbourne nearly 40 years ago". He also told his audience of his plans for trips to Italy, Egypt and Palestine.

The Temperance Hotel, Granby Street, Leicester

In 1872, at the age of 64 years, Thomas Cook embarked upon the one remaining challenge in organised travel. From his office at his Temperance Hotel, he planned and organised the first Round the World Tour. He personally led the tour and together with nine companions, set sail westward from Liverpool to New York in September 1872. They crossed America by train and stage coach, onwards over the Pacific Ocean by paddle steamer and proceeded to Japan, China and India. The journey home to England was via Aden, Egypt and the Suez Canal.

The epic journey took 222 days to complete and the cost was 270 guineas (£283.50) per person, a very considerable sum in 1872. The tour covered 29,000 miles of which 19,000 were spent at sea.

Thomas Cook's Rickshaw © Leicestershire County Council Museums, Arts and Records Service.
(In the foreground is Robert Ingle alias Thomas Cook)

Whilst in Yokohama, on his Round-the-World Tour, Thomas Cook purchased a rickshaw which he shipped back to England for the amusement of his three grandsons. In 1880, he presented it to the patients of the Towers Hospital, Leicester, "for them to use on their picnic days".

The rickshaw is now in the Snibston Discovery Park, Coalville.

4
Final Years

Thorncroft, 244 London Road, Leicester
(Now the Headquarters of the Leicestershire Branch Of The British Red Cross Society)

On 31 December 1878, Thomas Cook finally retired from his business at the age of seventy. Initially, he had hoped to obtain the lease of the then unoccupied Melbourne Hall, but that did not materialise and he decided to remain in his adopted town.

In readiness for his retirement, he had built the attractive red brick Italianate villa on London Road, in the Stoneygate suburb of Leicester, where he went to live with his wife and daughter. He continued to devote his energies to his temperance work and to Archdeacon Lane Baptist church in Leicester, where the family worshipped and were actively involved.

"Thorncroft"

The name chosen by Thomas Cook for his new home in retirement, was designed to link his Leicester home with his native Melbourne.

It was the late Reverend Tom Budge, a former minister of the Melbourne Baptist church and a respected authority on Thomas Cook, who explained to the author the story of *"Thorncroft"* - the carving of a thorn bush on the front elevation of the house, together with the name, linked the house to the quick-growing thorn bush so much favoured by the market gardeners of Melbourne. It also reminded the great pioneer of the tiny cottage where he was born, No. 9 Quick Close, Melbourne.

The former Bathroom at Thorncroft

Tragedy struck the Cook family on 6 November 1880 when Annie Elizabeth Cook, aged 34 years, was found by her father, drowned in her bath. Her death was due to the inhalation of fumes from a newly fitted gas water heater. The loss of their dearly loved only daughter was a terrible blow to Thomas and Marianne Cook; their intense grief caused great sadness throughout Leicester as well as nationally and across the world among her father's many acquaintances.

The United Baptist Chapel, Belvoir Street, Leicester (1845 - Joseph Hansom)

The funeral of Annie Cook took place on 12 November 1880. She was buried in Welford Road cemetery, Leicester. A large gathering attended, including the children from Archdeacon Lane, Baptist church where Annie had devoted so much of her life to the Sunday school. The civic dignitaries included the mayor, aldermen and councillors of the borough. The Mayor, Alderman John Bennett, was a fellow Baptist and attended the United Baptist Chapel where, for many years, he was the Sunday school superintendent. Thomas Cook later wrote of Alderman Bennett in an *In Memoriam* to his daughter: "Nothing effected him more than to witness the devotion of the children who wept at her tomb".

The chapel in Belvoir Street, known to generations of Leicester people as, "The Pork Pie Chapel" because of its unusual shape, became redundant in 1939 and since 1947 has formed part of the Leicester College of Adult Education.

The Bust of Annie Elizabeth Cook
(By permission of Horace E. Riddington)

In 1882, Thomas Cook proceeded to have built The Annie Cook Memorial Hall and Sunday school rooms in memory of his daughter. The building was situated close to the Baptist church where she had taught in the Sunday school. He also commissioned an Italian sculptor to carve a marble bust of Annie in Victorian style. The bust is in the custody of Buckminster Road Baptist church, Leicester.

The Eastgates Coffee House, Leicester
(1885 - Edward Burgess)

In November 1886, the fiftieth anniversary of the formation of the Leicester and Market Harborough Temperance Societies was celebrated. Thomas Cook arranged and compiled a 79 page book. *The Temperance Jubilee Celebrations 1886.* to commemorate the events which took place between the 13th and the 18th of November in both towns.

In it, Cook referred to, "The grand Coffee and Cocoa House Company of this Town (Leicester) and declared that, "The Company is one of the most illustrious of the benefits derived from the spread of Temperance principles". He had attended the very first meeting held to consider the advisability of forming the company and it was he who protested against the idea of, "making a coffee shop also a beer shop".

The Leicester Coffee and Cocoa House Company Limited was formed in 1877 and from the outset Thomas Cook was an ardent and influential supporter of the movement.

The High Cross Coffee House, High Street, Leicester

In all, 14 Coffee Houses were built in Leicester, the majority being open from 5.00am to 11.00pm daily. In addition to providing, "good tea, coffee, cocoa and eatables (without intoxicants) at low prices", the coffee houses were designed to provide comfortable dining rooms, reading rooms and billiards rooms. In general, they offered a real alternative to the public houses and beerhouses which Thomas Cook and others saw as a great source of temptation to working class people who had nowhere else to purchase refreshments.

The following extract is from the Company's price list in 1882:

Cup of coffee	1d
Pork pie	5d
Plate of potatoes	1d
Soup (basin)	2d
Ginger beer	1d

The Coffee Mills, Springfield Street, Market Harborough

The Market Harborough Temperance Society was formed in January 1836 and the Leicester Society in November of the same year. William Symington had held the office of president of the Market Harborough Society continuously throughout the first fifty years of its existence.

Thomas Cook recorded in his publication (p.70), that his friend, William Symington, was the first person to take the pledge when the Society was formed and that he himself was, "the last of the first group to be registered". Thomas Cook was the first secretary at Market Harborough and held the post for five years before moving to Leicester where he was corresponding secretary of the Leicester Society for many years until he became president. Only William Symington and Thomas Cook, of the original group of seven, lived to see the Golden Jubilee.

William Symington was the senior partner in the firm of W. Symington and Co. which was founded in 1839. The coffee mills were built in 1881.

The Bookcase presented to Market Harborough Baptist Church

Thomas Cook paid a return visit to Market Harborough in July 1887 upon the opening of the new schoolrooms at the Baptist church, having contributed £200 towards the total cost of £300. He also presented the church with an attractively designed bookcase, together with 300 books to be used by the children attending the Sunday School and meetings of the Band of Hope Union. The Leicestershire Band of Hope Union was set up in 1866 to deter young people, "from acquiring the appetite for alcoholic liquors".

The Pulpit in the Baptist Chapel, Barton-in-the-Beans

During March 1889, Thomas Cook reproduced, at his own expense, a publication entitled, *"The Barton Memorials: Works of Samuel Deacon.* Five small volumes of his works were bound into one book with an introduction by the Reverend John Rufus Godfrey, senior pastor at the Barton chapel from 1885-1907. The works were sold at a cost of 3s.6d. (17½p.) bound in cloth, or separately, in paper covers, at sixpence each.

Samuel Deacon jnr was co-pastor at Barton with his father, Samuel Deacon snr, for 33 years from 1779-1812. Samuel snr served for 52 years from 1760-1812 and his son for a total of 37 years from 1779-1816. The fame of Samuel Deacon jnr arose, not only from his preaching and his writings, but also from his great gift and skill as a clockmaker for which he gained a national reputation.

Memorial tablets to Samuel Deacon and his father are to be found in the chapel.

*The Day School adjoining the Baptist Chapel
Barton-in-the-Beans*

In the spring of 1889, Thomas Cook re-visited the Baptist chapels at Barton (31st March), Ashby-de-la-Zouch (3rd April) and Melbourne (4th April). He invited the members to tea which he provided, at his own expense, in the Sunday schools and day schools.

In the previous November, he had entered into correspondence with the Reverend William Hill, secretary of the General Baptist Missionary Society, to further his knowledge of the Barton Missionaries for whom he had the greatest admiration. He discovered that nine men and women had gone from Barton, as missionaries, to Orissa, in north-east India. He wrote at that time, "From the district under review many of the best men who ever went out to India have been raised up".

*The Deacon Memorial Library
Barton-in-the-Beans Baptist Chapel*

Whilst visiting the chapels at Barton and Melbourne, Thomas Cook presented both congregations with bookcases similar to the one he had given to the Market Harborough congregation two years earlier.

The Barton bookcase he called, "The Deacon Memorial Library" and it was duly placed in the minister's vestry.

Rothesay, Victoria Road, Leicester

During November 1889, Dr Henry Lankester became Mayor of Leicester. He and Thomas Cook were very close - they shared the same political beliefs, both being supporters of the Liberal party; they were fellow nonconformists and both were staunch members of the Temperance movement, Lankester being President of the Leicestershire Band of Hope Union.

He lived at Rothesay, Victoria Road, Leicester (now Nos 8-12 University Road), was a native of Poole, in Dorset and came to Leicester in 1854 where he set up a very successful medical practice.

Dr Lankester was family physician to the Cooks; it was he who was sent for when Annie Elizabeth died so tragically; it was also his sad duty subsequently to give evidence at the inquest.

Number 1 Chancery Street, Leicester

In 1890, the Fifth Annual Report of the Temporary Refuge for Homeless and Destitute Girls was published. The Refuge was situated at No.1 Chancery Street, Pocklington's Walk, Leicester and was opened in 1885. The cause was supported by Thomas Cook, both as an individual and as a member of Archdeacon Lane Baptist church. The total number of girls sheltered to 1 May 1890 was shown as 465.

The Baptist Memorial Cottages
High Street, Melbourne

Thomas Cook gave further evidence of his philanthropic nature when, in 1890, he undertook to pay for the building of 14 cottages and a mission hall at Melbourne, "for poor and deserving people belonging to the Baptist denomination". The architect chosen was Edward Burgess, of Leicester and London. The central clock on the building was made by William Christian Deacon, of Barton-in-the-Beans.

A trust was formed to select tenants for the cottages and to be responsible for the running of the venture. The inaugural meetings and services lasted an entire week. The formal opening took place on Tuesday, 10 March 1891, "with a keen wind and numberless snow-flakes dancing in the air - the outermost fringe of the fierce blizzard then raging over land and sea": *The Barton Church Magazine*, April 1891, Vol.l, No.4.

Atlas Chambers, Berridge Street, Leicester

The former Atlas Chambers were used by Edward Burgess as his Leicester office whilst his London office was located at No. 70 Guilford Street, Russell Square.

At the time he was commissioned to design Thomas Cook's memorial cottages at Melbourne, Burgess had become widely known in Leicester, principally as the architect to the Leicester School Board. In that capacity, he designed the majority of the new Board Schools in the town as well as the Desford Industrial School in the county (1881). He was also responsible for the building of most of the 14 coffee houses in Leicester.

Edward Burgess (1847-1929) was born in Leicester, the son of Alfred Burgess, a wool-stapler; the family belonged to the Quaker meeting.

Number 102 Regent Road, Leicester
(The former home of Alderman William Kempson)

A grand banquet was held at the Hotel Metropole, in London, on 22 July 1891, to commemorate the 50th anniversary of the commencement of the business founded by Thomas Cook. Owing to failing health, Thomas Cook was unable to attend and John Mason Cook was in the chair. The function was attended by almost 300 distinguished guests.

Leicester was represented by the Mayor, Alderman William Kempson. In his speech, the mayor said, "The inhabitants of Leicester are greatly indebted to Messrs Cooks for what they have done. They have contributed generously to the institutions of the Town and they are greatly esteemed by the inhabitants. I am glad to express the good feeling which is extended towards them".

Alderman Kempson (1805-93), a boot and shoe manufacturer, was the son-in-law of John Flower (1793-1861), the Leicester-born water-colour artist. He was mayor of Leicester on two occasions, the second in 1890-91 during his 86th year.

The Factory of Messrs Faire Brothers & Company
Southampton Street and Wimbledon Street, Leicester

The Leicester Temperance Society continued unabated with its work in 1891, 55 years after its formation. Thomas Cook continued as President and was ably supported by Watkin Lewis Faire, the Society's Vice-president and former Agent and Missionary.

Watkin Lewis Faire came to Leicester from Derby in 1850, he and his brother, George Robert Faire, founders of a business manufacturing boot and shoe laces (later elastic web and laces) in Granby Street. Their partnership was dissolved in 1871, WL Faire carrying on the business, assisted by three of his sons. The Wimbledon Street warehouse was opened in 1886. Watkin Lewis Faire, a close personal friend of Thomas Cook, in a tribute to Annie Cook, wrote:

> *May all the children whom she taught,*
> *To heaven at last be safely brought;*
> *And all who shared her friendship sweet*
> *Around thy throne in glory meet.*

The Baptist Church, Victoria Road, Leicester
(1856 - John Tarring)

Watkin Lewis Faire shared Thomas Cook's Baptist faith and worshipped at Victoria Road Baptist church, now the Seventh Day Adventist church, London Road. His temperance work was greatly admired over the years and in 1852 he was commended by Mr R. Charters, chief constable of Leicester, "For the valuable services rendered to the cause of the Town by his kind manner and indefatigable exertions, he had been the means of reclaiming some of the most abandoned and degraded drunkards".

Thorncroft, 244 London Road, Leicester

On the evening of 18 July 1892, Thomas Cook died suddenly and unexpectedly at his home, aged 83 years. His wife, Marianne, who had been such a loving and supportive companion, had died eight years earlier on 8 March 1884.

His final years alone at Thorncroft were not easy for him: he had lost his wife and daughter and the relationship with his son was less than harmonious; his sight had progressively deteriorated and he had almost total loss of vision. Despite these considerable set backs, Thomas Cook continued to draw strength from his church and the temperance movement to which he had never ceased to give of himself in return

The *Leicester Chronicle,* in an obituary dated 23 July 1892, said of him, "The total blindness which overcame him did not affect his spirits or prevent him from making an excursion to the Holy Land".

The Town Hall, Leicester
(1876 - Francis Hames)

Following the news of Thomas Cook's death, the flags were flown at half mast at the Temperance Hall and at Leicester's Town Hall which had been built 16 years earlier.

In an obituary of the Pioneer of Tourism, the *Leicester Daily Post* of 20 July 1892 reported, "As late as last week he was able to join a party of friends from Archdeacon Lane Chapel on a visit to Melbourne where he had erected some almshouses. He would have stayed there for a few days, but being anxious to vote for Mr Logan (the Liberal candidate) he returned on Wednesday (13th July) and went direct to the polling station at Knighton from the railway station". Thus it was that he departed in his adopted town rather than his place of birth.

Number 79 Princess Road, Leicester
(The Home of Watkin Lewis Faire)

Three days after the death of Thomas Cook, his friend and Temperance Society colleague, Watkin Lewis Faire, died at his residence at No. 79 Princess Road, Leicester, aged 73 years. He had retired five years earlier and the business was carried on by his three sons. The Leicester Temperance Society suffered a severe blow by the loss of its president and vice-president within the space of 72 hours.

The Grave of Thomas Cook

Thomas Cook's funeral took place at Welford Road cemetery, Leicester, on 25 July 1892, following a service at Archdeacon Lane chapel.

A vast crowd attended to pay respects to the memory of a man, "whose fame had spread all over the civilised world" (*Leicester Chronicle*, 20 July 1892). Twelve horse-drawn carriages followed the hearse, with the Mayor of Leicester, Alderman Thomas Wright, in the first carriage. With the mourners in the second carriage, was Dr Henry Lankester.

The funeral arrangements were in the hands of Messrs Gee, Nephew & Company; the carriages were supplied by William Burley, "Undertaker, Livery Stable Keeper and Cab Proprietor', of Evington Street, Leicester.

The Congregational Church, High Street, Market Harborough

A great many people travelled to Leicester to attend Thomas Cook's funeral, including representatives of the Market Harborough Temperance Society. The delegation consisted of the three vice-presidents: the Reverend Thomas Frederick Jerwood, Rector of Little Bowden, Samuel Symington and the Reverend William Edward Morris, Minister of the Congregational church.

The Market Harborough Congregational church was the work of the Leicester architect, William Flint, and was opened in 1844 as The Independent Chapel.

The Reverend Morris came to the church in 1872 and was minister there for 32 years (1872-1904).

The Home of Thomas Cooper, No.11 Churchgate, Leicester

The Reverend William Bishop, Minister of Archdeacon Lane Baptist chapel, gave the address at Thomas Cook's funeral and included these words: "His sympathy was with the struggling poor in the times of terrible distress in Leicester 50 years ago. It made him their Champion with such men as the late Thomas Cooper the chartist against the wrongs and injustices". Thomas Cooper, who was born in Leicester, was an early leader of the Chartist Movement. He died at his home in Lincoln on 15 July 1892 - three days before the death of Thomas Cook.

The Gladstone Building, Bishop Street, Leicester

Thomas Cook had been a supporter of the Liberal party throughout his life and his pioneering work in the field of travel and tourism had long been recognised by the great British statesman, William Ewart Gladstone (1809-1898).

Within days of the death of Thomas Cook, Gladstone's party won the general election and he became Prime Minister for the fourth time at the age of 82 years. He described Cook's achievements as ranking high among, "the humanising contrivances of the age". (*Leicester Daily Post*, 20 July 1892).

The Gladstone Building was designed by Edward Burgess and was formally opened as the town's Liberal Club by the Marquis of Ripon KG, on 31 May 1888.

The Vault of the Faire Family
Welford Road Cemetery, Leicester

The funeral of Watkin Lewis Faire took place immediately following Thomas Cook's interment, thus enabling the many representatives of the Temperance Society, both locally and nationally, to attend both funerals. The Reverend John Gersham Greenhough, Pastor of Victoria Road Baptist church, conducted the service and the employees from Southampton and Wimbledon Street factories were present.

The Inscription on the Faire Family Monument
Welford Road Cemetery, Leicester

Reference was made in the *Leicester Chronicle* of 23 July 1892 to Watkin Lewis Faire's early years in the town and in his capacity as Agent and Missionary for the Leicester Temperance Society. The obituary contained the following tribute: "For nearly six years Mr Faire continued to labour in this manner and during that time about 2000 pledges were taken. In 1851, during his first year's labours, he visited 3030 houses in the town".

On 21 July 1892, a meeting of the Leicester Temperance Society was held at the Temperance Hall. The chair was occupied by Dr Henry Lankester and generous tributes were paid to both Thomas Cook and Watkin Lewis Faire.

*The Offices of Thomas Cook & Son
Gallowtree Gate, Leicester*

In 1894. new offices were built for the firm in the centre of Leicester. The building was designed by the local architects, Messrs Goddard, Paget and Goddard and the design chosen was a pleasing Renaissance style with French and Flemish elements. The four terracotta panels, depicting the high points in the history of Thomas Cook & Son, are situated above the first floor windows and call for individual description. (pp.94-97).

Leicester to Loughborough Excursion - 5 July 1841

The left hand panel depicts Thomas Cook's first excursion train on its journey from Leicester to the Temperance meeting at Southfields Park, Loughborough. The train consisted of eight third-class carriages for the passengers and the band from Leicester, with a first-class carriage which was occupied by the guard. The engine was similar in design to George Stephenson's *Rocket* which he first used on the Liverpool to Manchester Railway in 1830.

Detail in the panel shows the passengers in open carriages (tubs) and a windmill clearly visible on one of the distant Charnwood hills.

The Great Exhibition - 1851

The second panel relates to the Great Exhibition which took place in Joseph Paxton's Crystal Palace, in Hyde Park, London, between May and October 1851 and was attended by more than six million people.

The construction of the railway engine and carriages had developed and improved, during the previous decade, as can be seen on the panel which shows a train and its passengers heading for the Exhibition.

The Crystal Palace was dismantled after the exhibition and reassembled at Sydenham as an Exhibition Centre and Concert Hall. It was totally destroyed by fire in 1936.

Egypt and the Nile - 1884

Panel number three relates to the great logistical operation undertaken by John Mason Cook in 1884. The British government had commissioned the firm of Thomas Cook & Son to be responsible for transporting an expeditionary force from Alexandria, up the Nile, to relieve General Charles Gordon and the British citizens trapped in Khartoum. The operation involved the movement of 18,000 troops and over 100,000 tons of supplies. General Gordon was killed on 26 January 1885, two days before the arrival of the relieving force, but John Mason Cook received the thanks of the government for his superhuman effort.

The panel, which shows the Nile and the Pyramids, plus a Nile steamer and a sailing craft, is also a reminder of the success of Cook's Nile service which was rapidly built-up after the opening of the Suez Canal in 1869.

The Firth of Forth Railway Bridge - 1891

The final panel on the offices depicts the great Forth Railway Bridge which was completed in 1890. The crossing of the Forth enabled Thomas Cook & Son to extend their travel and tourist arrangements up the east coast of Scotland.

A much more modern railway engine and carriages are shown speeding north, with the railway bridge on the left.

The year 1891 also served as a reminder that it was 50 years since Thomas Cook's first excursion. It was indeed a Golden Jubilee tribute to an early Victorian pioneer's great achievements.

Nithsdale House, Northampton Road, Market Harborough

Thomas Cook's great friend for over fifty years, William Symington, died at his home, Nithsdale House, Market Harborough, on 12 December 1898, aged 89 years. He had held the office of President of the Market Harborough Temperance Society from its outset in 1836 until his death - a period of 62 years.

In 1854, William Symington's firm was chosen to supply the allied armies engaged in the Crimean War (1854-56) with pea flour for the making of soup.

His funeral took place in Market Harborough on 18 December 1898 and the Reverend William E. Morris, Minister of the Congregational church where William Symington worshipped, officiated. William Symington left three sons, twenty-eight grandchildren and two great-grandchildren.

The Grave of John Mason Cook
Welford Road Cemetery, Leicester

Less than seven years after the death of Thomas Cook, his son, John Mason Cook, died on 4 March 1899 at his home, Mount Felix, Walton-on-Thames, aged 65 years.

John Mason Cook had proved himself a highly successful business man. Not only had he managed the firm with great skill, he expanded its operations with both flair and judgement. The previous year, he had been responsible for the visit of the German Emperor, Wilhelm II, to the Holy Land and became quite ill during the tour. He never recovered from the illness and died shortly after his return home.

Like his father, John Mason Cook was President of the Leicester Temperance Society at the time of his death, having succeeded his father in the office in 1892. The Reverend James Went, of Leicester, conducted the service at the cemetery and said of him: "He filled a place in the history of the 19th century".

The Store of Messrs Adderley & Company Limited
57-59 Market Place, Leicester

The funeral arrangements for John Mason Cook were carried out by the firm of Messrs Adderley & Co.

He was buried in the Anglican section of Welford Road cemetery and the *Leicester Advertiser* reported: "The vault where he was interred was a new one, it was lined with ivy and white lillies". Following the hearse, there were eight carriages with representatives from the Midland Railway Company and the Wycliffe Society for Helping the Blind in Leicester, whose work he had supported.

Thus it was that James Mason Cook was brought up as a Baptist, married in a Unitarian chapel and his funeral was conducted by an Anglican priest.

5
Modern Reminders

The Logo of the Thomas Cook Group

The logo of the Thomas Cook Group focuses upon the name of the man, born in a humble workman's cottage in Derbyshire, which is now known throughout the entire world.

The 1995 statistics of the Group reflect the staggering achievements of the firm started by the great pioneer: The Group employs over 12,000 staff world-wide who serve some 20 million customers each year; it has over 1300 wholly-owned and representative offices in over 100 countries around the world; in 1994, it announced a pre-tax profit of £60.7m and a turnover of £656.6m; gross sales were £17.1 billion.

> UPON
> 24th JUNE 1978,
> THE FIFTIETH ANNIVERSARY
> OF THE FOUNDING OF
> BRITISH JUNIOR CHAMBER,
> THIS PLAQUE WAS UNVEILED,
> TO COMMEMORATE
> THE FIRST EVER RAILWAY EXCURSION,
> FROM LEICESTER TO LOUGHBOROUGH,
> ORGANISED BY MR THOMAS COOK,
> ON 5th JULY 1841.
>
> PRESENTED
> BY LOUGHBOROUGH
> JUNIOR CHAMBER

The Commemorative Plaque
Loughborough Railway Station

The Loughborough Junior Chamber of Commerce appropriately celebrated the Golden Jubilee of the founding of the British Junior Chamber by unveiling a plaque, at Loughborough railway station, to commemorate Thomas Cook's first railway excursion to Loughborough in 1841.

The plaque was unveiled on 24 June 1978, a fitting tribute by the young men of the Loughborough Chamber to another young man who had made his mark in their town 137 years earlier, the implications of which were to be of world-wide significance.

The Blue Plaque at Thorncroft

On 25 May 1978, the Lord Mayor of Leicester, Councillor Albert Watson, unveiled a plaque in memory of Thomas Cook at his former home, Thorncroft, 244 London Road, Leicester.

The plaque was the first in a series of blue plaques, commissioned by Leicester City Council, to commemorate the city's famous forbears. Mr Alan Kennedy, Chief Executive of the firm of Thomas Cook and Son, in thanking the council for having honoured Thomas Cook, remarked: "He opened up the world for the ordinary man and woman".

The Open Book on the Grave of Thomas Cook
Welford Road Cemetery, Leicester

The grave of Thomas Cook was refurbished and given a complete facelift by the world renowned travel firm in 1975.

An additional open book was placed on the grave, as a tribute, giving details of his major achievements, thus enabling visitors, who come from many parts of the world, to appreciate the very considerable contribution which Thomas Cook made in terms of 19th century progress.

The epitaph is truly apt:

> *"He brought travel to the millions"*

> THOMAS COOK BORN
> 22ND. NOVEMBER 1808
> IN QUICK CLOSE
> OPPOSITE THESE COTTAGES
> FOUNDER OF MODERN
> TRAVEL
> DIED 18TH. JULY 1892

The Plaque on the Mission Hall at Melbourne

A plaque on the Mission Hall, which forms part of the Memorial Cottages complex at Melbourne, informs visitors that Thomas Cook was born in the house opposite, No.9 Quick Close.

The cottages are still in use and continue to be managed by a local committee of trustees as they have been throughout the years since Thomas Cook first drew up the Deed of Trust in 1890. It is no longer necessary to have a Baptist connection to be considered for a tenancy of one of the cottages.

When opened in 1891, the cottages were a far cry from the humble cottage in which Cook spent his early years and to-day serve to perpetuate his memory.

Archdeacon Lane Memorial Baptist Church
Buckminster Road, Leicester

The old Archdeacon Lane Baptist church, where Thomas Cook and his family worshipped, was demolished in 1938, followed by the demolition of the Annie Cook Memorial Hall and Sunday school in 1970, to make way for redevelopment of the site.

A new Baptist church was built in Buckminster Road in 1939. A plaque in the entrance reads:

> *This tablet was erected by the members of*
> *the Baptist Church in Archdeacon Lane, Leicester to*
> *perpetuate the memory of that place of worship.*
>
> *The old chapel was demolished in 1938 in connection*
> *with a street widening scheme and the proceeds of the sale*
> *of the premises provided this church and school.*

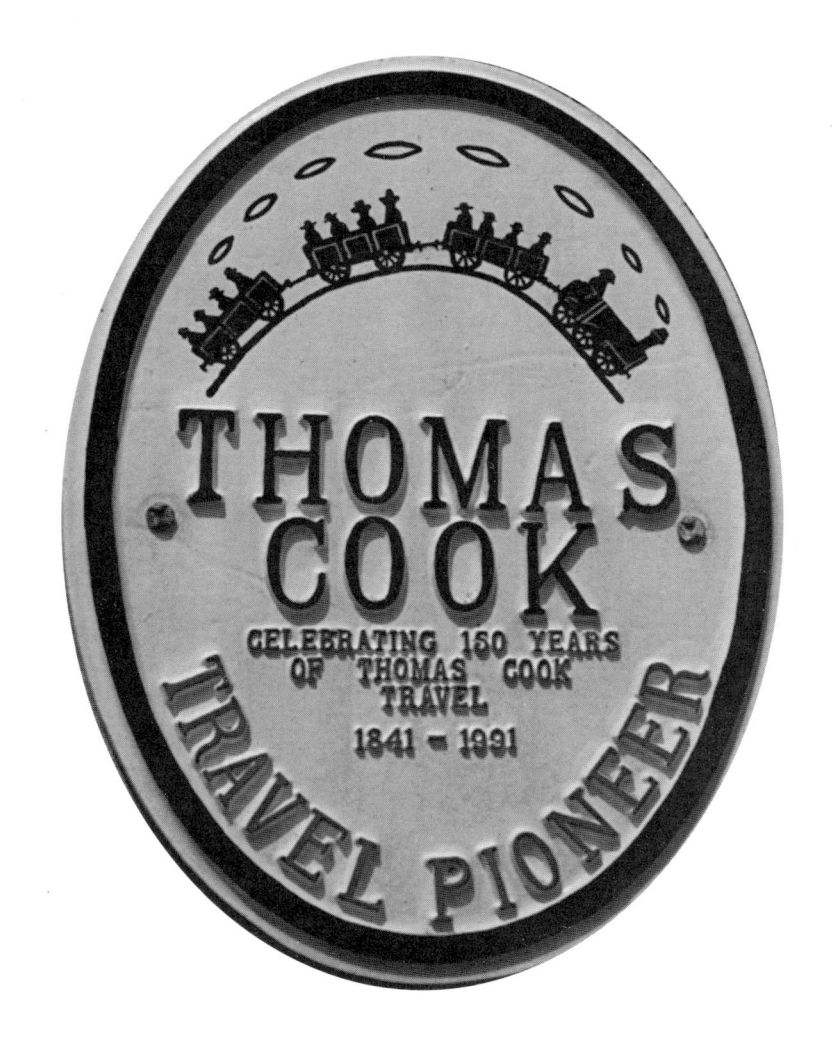

The Plaque celebrating 150 years of Thomas Cook Travel

During 1993, twelve commemorative plaques were made to mark the 150th anniversary of Thomas Cook's first railway excursion.
The Leicester Victorian Society promoted the project and Leicester Environment City gave a grant to cover the cost. The design was by Inger McKenzie and the cast iron plaques were made by Chris Ludlow. The plaques have been placed on buildings in Leicester, Loughborough, Barrowden, Market Harborough, Kibworth Harcourt, Belvoir Castle and in Thomas Cook's native village of Melbourne.

The Statue of Thomas Cook by James Butler RA
London Road, Leicester

On 14 January 1994, a statue of Thomas Cook was unveiled by his great great grandson and namesake. Situated on the corner of London Road and Station Street, Leicester, it is cast in bronze and was commissioned by Leicester City Council with assistance from British Railways Community Unit and Thomas Cook International Ltd. It marked the centenary of the death of Thomas Cook and stands, appropriately, close to the site of the former Campbell Street station where it all began.

Robert Ingle alias Thomas Cook

The spirit of Thomas Cook lives on as the new millennium draws near. Since 1983, Robert Ingle, of Leicester, has played the role of Thomas Cook at a variety of functions, in authentic dress and with an in-depth knowledge of the character which led him to write the biography: *Thomas Cook of Leicester.*

Appendices

Some of those who knew Thomas Cook and rest near to him in Welford Road Cemetery, Leicester

Welford Road Cemetery, Leicester
(1849 - Hamilton & Medland)

Appendix I

The Reverend Joseph Foulkes Winks

A mere 75 yards away from Thomas Cook's grave lies his friend and mentor, Joseph Foulkes Winks, who baptised him into the Baptist faith and had a profound influence on the shaping of the early years of his life.

Joseph Winks was a printer of Baptist publications in Leicester for almost 40 years; he died on 28 May 1866.

Appendix II

John Ellis

John Ellis was a native of Leicester and a successful farmer and industrialist. He was a Liberal member of the town council and went on to represent the Borough in parliament(1848-52).

He was chairman of the Midland Railway Company from 1849 to 1858 and it was during that time that he worked closely with Thomas Cook. He died on 26 October 1862.

Appendix III

The Reverend Samuel Wigg

Samuel Wigg was a colleague of Thomas Cook in the Leicester Temperance Society and accompanied him to the Rural Festival, at Cossington, in September 1848, where he was one of the speakers. They were joint secretaries of the society in 1849.

Wigg was the pastor of the Baptist church in Friar Lane, Leicester, for 40 years until his death on 18 July 1861. His son, the Reverend Samuel Wathen Wigg, became vicar of Anstey, Leicestershire.

Appendix IV

Thomas William Hodges

Thomas Hodges was the father of John Mason Cook's wife Emma. He was an elastic web manufacturer and became a town councillor, in Leicester, in 1859; an alderman in 1862, he was mayor of the borough for the three successive years 1865-67.

At the age of 67 years, he died at his residence in Leicester on 1 October 1874.

Appendix V

John Bennett

John Bennett, who was born in Leicester, was a corn factor and became a Liberal representative on the borough council on 17 December 1866. He was mayor of Leicester in successive years, 1879-80. In November 1880, he represented the council and citizens of Leicester at the funeral of Annie Eizabeth Cook.

He died at his home in Princess Road, Leicester, on 2 November 1906.

Appendix VI

Doctor Henry Lankester

Henry Lankester, the friend, fellow temperance worker and physician to Thomas Cook, had six sons and one daughter. Four of his sons were doctors. He became a town councillor in 1879 and was mayor in 1889.

He died at his residence in Salisbury Road, Leicester, on 30 January 1902 - 24 hours after the death of his elder brother in Lewisham, London.

The Family Tree of the three generations of the Cook Family involved in the firm's business of Travel & Tourism

Thomas Cook
Born 22 November 1808 at Melbourne, Derbyshire
Married 2 March 1833 Marianne Mason of Barrowden
Died 18 July 1892 at Leicester

John Mason Cook
Born 13 January 1834 at Market Harborough, Leics
Married 27 December 1861 Emma Hodges of Leicester
Died 4 March 1899 at Walton-on-Thames

Frank Henry Cook
Born 25 September 1862 at Leicester
Married 21 June 1894 Beatrice Elliott Lindell of St Louis, Missouri, USA.
Died 25 December 1931 at Wonersh, Surrey.

Ernest Edward Cook
Born 4 September 1865 at Camberwell
Died 14 March 1955 at Bath.

Thomas Albert Cook
Born 25 June 1867 at Camberwell
Married 24 Aug 1900 Margaret Russell
Died 5 September 1914

1928 Frank and Ernest retired and sold the business to the International Sleeping Car Company, Wagons-Lits of Belgium.

1972 Thomas Cook & Son was bought by a consortium consisting of the Midland Bank, Trust House Forte and the Automobile Association.

1992 The German Westdeutsche Landesbank and the LTU Group acquired the Thomas Cook Group from the Midland Bank Group.

Bibliography

Banner, John W.	Discovering Leicester	Leicester	1991
Brandwood, Geoff & Cherry, Martin.	Men of Property	Leicester	1990
Brendon, Piers.	Thomas Cook	London	1991
Davies, J.C. & Brown, Michael.	Victorian Harborough	Buckingham	1980
Deacon, Samuel.	Preacher, Pastor, Mechanic.	Leicester	1888
Devonshire, Duchess of.	Chatsworth	Derby	1994
Devonshire, Duchess of.	Chatsworth Garden	Derby	1993
Elliott, Malcolm.	Victorian Leicester	Chichester	1979
Hartopp, Henry.	Roll of the Mayors & Lord Mayors of Leicester 1205-1935	Leicester	1935
Hewitt, P.A.	The Deacon Family of Leicestershire Clockmakers	Ticehurst	1987
Ingle, Robert.	Thomas Cook of Leicester	Bangor	1991
Jones, T.L.	Ashby-de-la-Zouch Castle	London	1984
Osborne, S.C.	The First Two Hundred Years Hinckley Baptist Church	Hinckley	1966
Pevsner, Nikolaus Second edition revised by Williamson, Elizabeth.	The Buildings of England Leicestershire and Rutland	Handmondsworth	1984
Powell, Reverend Vaughan Second edition revised by Hill, Val.	The Baptists of Billesdon	Leicester	1995
Pudney, John.	Thomas Cook	London	1953
Todd, John R.	By the Foolishness of Preaching	Barton-in-the-Beans	1993
Wooldridge, A.D.F.	Market Harborough Baptist Church History 1830-1980	Market Harborough	1980

Thanksgiving Service

A Thanksgiving Service was held at the graveside of Thomas Cook on 7 July 1991. The service was arranged by the Leicester Group of the Victorian Society, to commemorate the 150th Anniversary of his first excursion from Leicester to Loughborough, on 5 July 1841.

> **This Copy**
>
> OF THE
>
> **Memoir of Mr. Deacon**
>
> IS
>
> **PRESENTED BY MR. THOMAS COOK,**
>
> OF
>
> **Thorncroft, Leicester,**
>
> TO
>
> *Mrs Blower*
>
> *Bagworth*
>
> Mr. COOK is desirous of presenting a Copy of this Book to every General Baptist Minister, Local Preacher, and General Baptist Sunday School Library in the district; also to the poorer Members of the Churches, and the descendants of former Members of the Churches, within a radius of twenty miles from Barton.

A Presentation by Thomas Cook

Extracted from a copy of the Memoir of Samuel Deacon which was presented by Thomas Cook to Mrs Sarah Blower of Bagworth, Leicestershire. The book is in the possession of her great grandchildren Peter Willett and Mrs Sheila Timmington.